Monty Reid

CRAWLSP

New and
Selected Poems

Anansi

for David and Corey

First published in 1993 by
House of Anansi Press Limited
1800 Steeles Avenue West
Concord, Ontario
L4K 2P3
(416) 445-3333

Canadian Cataloguing in Publication Data

Reid, Monty, 1952-
Crawlspace: new and selected poems

Poems.
ISBN 0-88784-539-8

I. Title.

PS8585.E603C7 1993 C811'.54 C93-093587-X
PR9199.3.R453C7 1993

Cover design: Brant Cowie/ArtPlus Limited
Author photograph: Patricia Wood
Printed and bound in Canada

House of Anansi Press gratefully acknowledges the support of the Canada Council, Ontario Ministry of Culture, Tourism, and Recreation, Ontario Arts Council and Ontario Publishing Centre in the development of writing and publishing in Canada.

Contents

Acknowledgments

Over the years, many people have helped. Thank you to Doug Barbour and Stephen Scobie, Bert Almon, Tom Wayman, George Melnyk, Pat Lane, David Spalding and David Arnason. Robert Kroetsch, Aritha van Herk and Robert Hilles have seen various manifestations of these poems come and go and their support has been unstinting.

To the staff at NeWest, Thistledown, Longspoon, and especially Dennis Johnson at Red Deer College Press, your hard work is much appreciated. Thank you to Donald G. Bastian and his colleagues at Anansi for herding this project through the press. Thanks also to everyone at the Museum. And to the Acoustic PotLuck Music Festival Society, it's in G.

A special thank-you to Don McKay for his care and insight. And to Pat Wood, as before, I continue to be in debt.

from

Karst Means Stone

To Start With

we pick our starts
out of forgetfulness

three things
— a boy fell into a well
and his father after him
— a man ground under a
windmill's wheel
— the river flooding

a way to begin

at fifty-five
he can't call what he writes
a diary, things not fixed
in each day's history

all through
he keeps coming back
with details, forgotten earlier
each memory a starting over

this beginning again
the advantage of memoir
cutting into history here

or there

eating off a cellar door,
wrestling, the names,
inconsequentials

memories tended

and dis-tended
as if there were some ideal sequence
against which these things
the camels,
Krentze's bin,

are
just enough
for comparison

which is what beginning is

Handles

"In 1900 Katrina's dad passed away. I was asked to make the handles for his coffin, which I really did so gladly. Because of the funeral our marriage had to be delayed again."

I walk around with a dead man
in my mouth. She asked me to put
the handles on and I remember
how the pale wood curled out
of the holes as the screws wormed in.
And then she said you must not
see Katrina til the mourning ends.
I was never at ease with him
and now, even dead, he's a weight
to contend with. I remember him
wrestling at Easter, how good he was,
leaning into the circle and later
he walked with a stoop we said
came from wrestling too much,
not old age. Now I'm pinned
to the mat of my tongue.

The screws bore a hole
and fill it: security. She said
to wait is only decent.
I could give him a fall.
Have a handle break in the middle
of an aisle but no, they'll hold.
And later, when we carry
this corpse out together
and bury it under dirt and stones
my tongue will lift again
in my mouth, dancing
beyond the hold of pain.

Photos

"I left Sterling, Colorado, went back to Kansas. My wife took the children to Kamishin to have pictures taken. I had asked her to have them taken and arrange them so that I can find a place on the photo too. She sent them to me and I had them done with myself also sitting with them."

She took the children to Kamishin
to have pictures made. I sent
the money home. This family
arrangement, the separation.

The children sprawl out of her lap
in sailor suits and lace dresses.
There is a light space for me
to be placed in. The photographer's brushes

to touch me in; there is one
in Fort Collins. A picture
to bring us together. It will
surprise her mother, our

friends, the cousins I work for.
They'll say it's an old one
but I'll date it in town.
They know I haven't been home

and I haven't. Sometimes my body
fits into spaces not made for it.
I won't pretend. She leans
backward against the weight

of the smallest daughter;
it will seem she leans on me
if the man can do it.
He should place me

standing sideways. My shoulders
may be too big. I'll
let him decide. A dozen
if I like them, paying well.

We can say we're together
or have been recently.
It will be some consolation
for these blank spaces.

The Current Talk

"We found to be separated from each other held temptations for both of us. There were always those who gossip and start rumors to cause problems between a couple."

the current talk
avoids me
knowing I'm
its center
not noticing
I'm in the room
they remark
how my absence
is filled

her letters
in my pocket
a charm
against words
spoken
at suppertables
bland food
teasing tongues
to indiscretion

I live from
rumor to rumor
the way my neighbors
live   hand
to mouth

Into Continuity

"In the fall of the year a sad tragedy took place on a farm west of Duval. The Kuxhouse's second daughter took her life by hanging. The present pastor would not bury a suicide so I was asked to perform the funeral service."

"I speak after the manner of men
            because of the infirmity of your flesh."

what I chose to read them at the grave
not
            "for sin shall not have dominion
            over you: for ye are not under
            the law, but under grace"

two verses before.

Kuxhaus, Kuxhouse
there is no motive
for the change
but the change is there.
The "e" hung on, silently,
the name becomes the place
it lives in.

When they found her body
in the bin in the middle
of the field, the light
through knotholes or gaps
in the warped shiplap and
the sky filled with swallows
that rattle up from the mudded
eaves, she was turning slightly
on the shifting air.

No one wanted to touch her
and the church didn't want
to say anything at all.
Later that year it was dissolved
and I began these memoirs,
stepping into continuity
without sound.
I cut her down.
I spoke at the grave.
And I can still see the way
she dangled useless in the air
the last "e" this language
won't pronounce.

Seeding

"The weather this spring was very dry, had high winds for seven weeks so that many farmers lost their crops by soil drifting, some reseeded again but then only Russian thistle grew, so that there was no crop."

last fall
the weeds tumbled
across the fields
like refugees

they collect at the fences
but don't burn
and by then the ground
is full of their seeds anyway

it's as if the land
sprouts your memories
even though you planted wheat

The Ostensive Method

"In the spring of 1945, April 27, Felix's second daughter was born, named her Wilma Marlene."

you can make
no assumptions

I take her hand
trace letters
in the palm

and she thinks
I'm tickling

or, pointing
things out

der Stuhl
der Tisch
das Puppchen

the first definition
is to touch
with the finger

a problem
of repetition
and what is at hand

until Felix's wife
takes her
"don't dad
she hasn't
learned
them in
English yet"

later
she puts her doll
in my hands

and says over
and over again
all the
wrong words

Karst Means Stone

"My life's experiences are written in this book, from my childhood to the end of my life . . . I was now 76 years old, my wife 72 years."

My name is Samuel Karst.
My wife: Katherina Yauk.
My sons: Alex, Constantine,
Samuel, Edward, Gus, Felix,
in that order.
Alex and Constantine dead.
My daughters: Amalie and Agatha.

the ellipsis
the horizon's crack
the poem slips through

I came to this country
three times.
I worked on the sewer,
on the oil tanks,
as a blacksmith,
as a farmer.

the name, Karst,
means stone
the face cut
runnelled
as limestone

My name is Samuel Karst.
There is nothing different
about this country.

his grandchildren touch
the cracked skin
their fingers cool
as water

The Sparrows

I never thought it could go on
so long, this death drawing across
her perpetual skin, the breath rasping
in her throat like a knife on stone.
The room is dull, the patched blinds
drawn through the light. Outside,
in the tree by the window the sparrows
are a thousand pips of noise
and here, bird-like, her fingers
pluck the quilts under which
she lies. Her eyes have already
that clarity you expect of the dead
or the half-dead.

The boys
say it would be better
to happen quickly. Sometimes
I imagine that the boys are still
at home. I always notice the round
black eyes of the sparrows, how
there was no way to keep the light
out. But I was wrong. Felix showed
me how the eyes close, the way the skin
draws interminably together.

Outside
the birds
are suddenly gone.

It is as if

it is as if
there is no difference
in the entries of his speech
into this country

no ground marked
that could not be marked
in another language

in the entries of a diary
of another place

he arrives
and it is as if
he never arrives

or is always
not quite getting there

there is no place in the memoir
you can point, say
look, this could only
be written here

it is as if
he wrote this
waiting for a place to happen

like an accident

it is as if
as if

from

The Life of Ryley

The Road Back and Forth to Ryley

The mist splits open for light the way the heart
is parted for clarity. On the fields
at the edge of town white-tail browse
dark air damp on their pelage. Morning
edges down the road behind us and we've
forgotten the camera, as we always do when
deer are there, but always have it when dead skunks
and porcupines lie on the shoulders, entrails
plucked by magpies, ravens, unphotogenic crows.
Or we're late for work and can't stop.
The deer lift their heads but don't run
and the ground goes fluent with dawn.

Or the dark in mid-winter.
Through the moraine at Cooking Lake
where glaciers off the mountains and the shield
met and ground slowly into one another.
Now the snow through aspens that cover
the hummocks of till. Cones of light.
Drifts climb from the ditches, sprawl
unself-consciously over the road and we follow
the snowplow at thirty mph not
seeing anything except the blue light
diffract in white.

The girls they have for flagmen wave you down.
Euclids belly along the roadbed, the dirt
all ruts or hung in the air like an allergy
and it's summer, the girls in hardhats and
haltertops, shoulders flushed with
sun. All you can see is dust. Or farther
past the construction, where heat wraps the highway
in cellophane, the way things are packaged
so you don't see what you've got til you've paid
for it. But I could drive this road
blindfolded.

The city hoists itself into light
block by block on threads of smoke
and the traffic thickens, bumper to bumper
all the way in from Sherwood Park and when one stops
everybody does. If you were with me
you'd be nervous, stiffening every time
someone merged ahead of us, your foot
pumps an imaginary brake.
At night, from Ryley
the city's glare floats on the horizon like the nest
of a waterbird. In the morning, driving,
it disappears.

Commuters

Heat opens eyes
on the windshield.

Your breath hits it
fogs and disappears.

The cold comes up
to the glass to
look in.

Last night at the upstairs
window you melted a hole
in the frost with your fingertips.
They came away white
as headlights.

Now
we wait for the van
to warm up
you shiver
in the apparent air

while cars approach
and vanish
on the street

and in this blind magic
we also disappear.

Meeting Hutterites

i

Rumor has it
they're inbred
they bring in
males to lock
in the colony
shed overnight
with all the
cross-eyed girls.

New blood.

And now
at the door
a girl in
a black skirt

jars of honey
in a tray.

ii

I remember how
my uncle axed the heads
off chickens
the spouting neck
beating
into shed walls.

I was always afraid
of the bird flying
into me.

And now they come
to the door
with their sack
of headless frozen birds.

The wind lifts
their scarves like
wings.

iii

An accident we saw once:

a two-ton
upside down in the ditch
with bags of fertilizer broken
and spread on the road like dead birds.

We could smell gas leaking as we pried
at the doors with a crowbar.
Inside, they
were pounding their hands against the metal.

When we got them out there was blood
on their black pants.
It was cold.
They were shaking and went back to scrape
the sacks off the road with borrowed shovels.

iv

Black

they stand
in the snow
like print
on a page.

Is that why I think of death?

Once when the school
toured the colony
the Hutterite kids
followed us around

singing.

The Last Daughter Leaves Home

Drawn
as a wishbone
is drawn

to those
known or
secret wishes

this family
is spread.

Susan
in a chicken joint
these faces
greased by tears

in a spattered
kitchen and
for minimum
wage

her
hands pluck
that slim bone
from my chest.

Spring Ease

In March the waxwings picked the shrivelled berries
off the ash tree. The cat twitched at the window
and the gray clouds edged under the horizon.
Slow month. Now the birds turn on the wind
that whips the clouds from the sky, the cat
scratches at the door. The girl, whose eyes
also are gray, who says the kitchen's hot,
lets the cat out as she herself leaves for a walk
among the hills, hunting for crocus. April.
May. The boys work overtime. She sits on the hill's
south face, a flower in her hand.
Now there is only desire, warm
ground. Her eyes follow the cloud over
the hills. Sun and wind flush her face
as love would. In the kitchen she sets the plates
on the tablecloth covered with flowers.
The men come in from the field
and don't notice.

Cousins

I don't remember the names
of all the parts I handed up
to Brian as he lay half in the dusty hole.
Twelve years old and only wanting to be sure
that I was helping as he pulled
the beater bars from the clogged belly
of the old pulltype. They rotated backwards,
barley caught between them and the combine
had to stop every hundred yards just
to let them clear. Now we have it
in the yard: apart.
He had a plastic mask
over his face because he was allergic
to barley dust and I remember coughing too
and getting a rash on my elbows and neck.

Years later, and I still don't know
the names of things. We sit around
the suppertable and recall the few times
I helped on the farm, how I'd sulk
or try to sic the dog on the chickens
when they told me just to keep out of the way.
We examine the various partings
how I've worked in the city
for three or four years now and
Brian, like he does every time I see him,
has to ask, what was it
you said you did?

The Disposal of Hazardous Wastes

The cultivator unfolds the earth: old
letters. We read them again and again.
The shovels turn the worms up and they lie
like veins on the surface, stunned by light.
Dirt runs through them like blood.
When they move the birds get them,
pluck them in their beaks like string.

Here in the yard a nest of mouths
they stitch together. They stand
on the lip of twigs and dangle the worms.
Drop them, preen, and are gone.
They feed all day. The next they
follow the sprayer across the second
quarter, its booms spread out
for balance: tightrope
of earth.

The air takes the spray apart
and even though there is no wind
we can smell it. It hangs
in the yard like the must
of old papers bound with twine
and stacked in the basement.
What is it we write
to ourselves?

The day after, we found the gawky
bodies on the lawn. Plucked out,
veins blue with pesticide, transparent
skin. We picked them up and
threw them in the ditch. A cat
will probably find them. And as we
walked from the house to wherever
we could hear the birds, their songs
tumble over and over
out of the air.

Groceries

The packages slide
past: cellophane and tin,
and the teller pokes the register
the way she'd poke a fat
man in the ribs. You're
missing one; she totals
up our bones.

I remember peaches.
I took one off the store
display and ate it as we
filled our cart.
The store detectives caught
us at the checkout.
They never said much
but I could taste that peach
for days.

The Ladies Gossip

Edna tells Molly and Molly tells
Chrissie and Chrissie tells Ida and Nora
gets it from her. So Nora tells
Susan and Susan tells Rita and Rita
tells Katherine and Bev.
Meanwhile Molly phoned Josephine
who passed it on to Flo and Muriel
who told Louise and Val and Shirley.
Shirley told the girls at the office
and Louise told Wendy. Wendy told
Margaret who told Joyce who
told Leona. Gail rubbered in
when Leona called Alice and she
told Carol. Carol told Mildred
and Mildred even told her mother.
Her mother told Irene and Myrtle
when she had them in for coffee.
Alice told Mona. Myrtle told
Janice but Janice heard it a long
time ago. Irene told Ethel who
told Sylvia who told Diane who told
Donna who told the other Donna
who told Yvonne who told
her younger sister. Ethel
told Rita again but Rita
said she heard it different. Mona
finally decided to tell someone
and Audrey was so shocked she told
Dorothy who told Violet and Anne.
Anne told Betty and Daphne. It
got the whole town talking.

Betty told Agnes and Agnes told Wilma.
Somehow Miriam heard it. Ruth
found out from Cathy and told
Kay who told Bonnie. What
a bunch of gossips said Bonnie.
She told June. June told Darlene
who told Gloria. Gloria told Gwen
and Gwen told Sherry and Sherry went
and told Barb and Barb told Tracy
and Tracy said no you've got
the whole thing wrong. So Barb
went back and told Sherry
who told Gwen who told Gloria
and someone told Pat
and even I heard it
and now since it's nice
to know how things get started
around here
I'm telling you.

Loose Tooth

Corey wouldn't let us touch
his first loose tooth
for over two months,
not trusting our hands
for small enough motions.

He wiggled it with his tongue
and fingers, til it hung
by a thread, but couldn't
bring himself to pull
it out.

And then one day in the city
he swallowed it, with
a mouthful
of Big Mac.

Crawlspace

Why they built this house
with no basement is beyond me.
Just this space between the planks
of the floor and the ground, damp.
I go down on my belly to check
the pipes, the wiring and two
feet above me the kids run.
They take it for granted
there's nothing under them.
The way leaves fall. Except
in January when winter sits here
like an animal and the pipes freeze
and frost blooms on the foundation.
Then when they run they run
softly. But now the spiders
are the only things scared,
legging it out of crevices.
And I'm lying here with the troublelight
looking at the pipes, listening
to the lives passing overhead
and under me, where I wish
I had a basement, comes the rustling
breath of an animal that lives
in the ground and every time we move,
moves.

Pouring Cement at Helen's

Rye and water, half and half
or rye straight. Helen makes the drinks
and sets them on the table.
Today we poured cement around her house,
sidewalk and patio, and tomorrow
if it's cool we'll take the forms off.
For now though we're finished.
Floated, trowelled, the edging done,
a pattern put on the surface with a broom
so no one slips on it. We sit
around the table as Helen
and her daughters do the dishes,
scraping scraps into the garbage.
We slouch in our seats, or tilt
the chairs back, precarious as wheelbarrows.

And later Helen compares this house
to others she's lived in. No heat,
no water, no sidewalks. How the kids
all slept in one room, the parents
in another and the rest was kitchen.
How one night in February she got up
and had to go to the bathroom which was,
on that farm, about ten miles away, it
seemed like, and because nobody would get up
and go with her she thought she'd go
instead in the slop-pail under the sink.

The floor was freezing and she didn't
wear shoes because she didn't want anyone
to hear her. She got the half-full five
gallon pail out and instead of just sitting
on it she tried to hold it tilted under her
so she could pee against the side
and not make noise. It slipped.
She fell into the slop running on the floor,
the peels, the grease, the dirty water
dripping through the trapdoor
into the cellar and already freezing.
She had to wash her ass in the dishpan
and it took her most of the night
to scrape the mess off the floor.
But no one woke up.

We are thrown back in our chairs
roaring and Gary overbalances and slams
against the wall and after that
we all sit, in this house full of warmth
and light and modern comfort,
with four legs firmly on the ground.

Homecoming '79

All the people who come home are old.
In the afternoon the old men sat
in the shade beside the legion,
watched for out-of-province plates,
while the ladies served coffee and date squares
at the community hall. The old-timers
played ball and won.
All day we shake the hands of people
who knew us when we were that high;
they come home to reclaim us.
We smile and don't remember.

At night, in the weird shadows
from three bulbs strung across the ceiling
of the tent they're using for a bar
we watch the people press in
watch for a face lit by heat or
beer or ghosts, some
grin to recognize.
But there are none, except Jack
who ran a truck from Ryley to the city.
I moved these people he says
Edmonton, Medicine Hat, Flatbush . . . away.
As soon as one left they all wanted to go.
Now they're here and some of them never
did pay me. I always thought
I'd buy another truck and move
some of them home.
His hands hold on to the back of a chair
like a steering wheel and in the vague
familiarity of generations, faces our
grandparents knew, here now for the dead
myths of a small town, the conversation
hammers like an engine in the hall.

from

The Dream of Snowy Owls

Après-Ski

i

nobody
is more lonely
than the driver

of a car full of sleepers
coming home from a trip
to the mountains

they fold their jackets into
pillows
and lean on one another
and never crowd the driver

night bends on the highway, full
of snow, static
for the radio, a place

to fill with light, and the
sleepers, dreaming, their
feet hot, wake

and ask, how
much further

ii

even sleeping, a body is not perfect
of itself

                they lie on their bruises
and have to move. it's like that:

you drive they said, and we'll
keep you awake

now
their throats get sore, the soft
rasp of nylon against
nylon, plastic zippers

the small
movements of a body finding
comfort, leaning
in an enclosed space

against the drift of other
bodies
against the door

iii

snow in the headlights

blind transparent fish
that glow in pools
in the belly of the rock

you strike a match
and they come gaping

to the surface

iv

green of dashlights. the wheel
tugs in his hands.
out
of the mountains, the car
dreams direction.

moonlight, fields of shallow water, her
hand falling, accidentally,
in his lap

all misread: body
moon, horizon, the hand
not held

and his legs, sleeping
because he will not move them

v

it is the accidental
the lapse, that keeps
him awake. after

so many miles the light
is all glare. traffic
glows like fish he has

only imagined
black pools under the
mountain

they wake in the city
the light, or the rhythm
gone, and say

you must be tired
are we here already

disappear
into the dark house, with
skis, boots, half-empty
cases of beer, as

fish
disappear into rock

vi
days later

it swims in them, the stiffness
the brilliant snow, all the ways
of recollection

held
like coffee mugs in a tiny kitchen

you could've switched off
they tell him
if you were tired

his cup is full of
grounds
collected
in his hand

as any
plan
an
aching in the legs

he doesn't really mind
the driving he says

reaches out
for one more cup

R-value

spun glass, separate fibre upon
fibre, glass full of air

as this room is filled with intricate
flesh, moonlight

sifting, glass in the cloud
caught in pockets of dead

air, the exchange of nothing
save desire

across the insular, pink
batts fit among studs of

bone, friction, light
across all this the

body's heat
itching at the spun

beauty, at the empty and
translucent room

My Wife Paints Her Fingers

i

loner. a bandit sneaks
up on a crowd. in the suburbs
of the hand he goes quietly
insane. she should paint
a mask across his eye.
when you make a gun with
your fingers he's the hammer.

ii

when your fingers do the walking
he walks. let's wobble this job.
he leans against the lips
like the unemployed at a wicket.
he was looking for a job
when he found this one.
he touches the dial of a phone
the way he touches the body's
gossip. kiss and tell.
in the bar-rooms of the nose
he points you out and talks
up union. he loves a profit
margin the way he never
loved you.

iii

regal. a queen in front
of the bastard's firing squad.
her ladies lean on her
for support and protection.
she says vive la france and fuck you.
when they drop a hood
over her head you still
can feel her eyes.

iv

the one most given away. she
sneaks out of the castle
in golden slippers and tries
to lose herself in the crowd.
but nothing can hide the beauty
or the lust. sometimes she
can't give it away.
paint her red and she's embarrassed.

v

at the end of the table
dissent. a little left
wing. the standing committee
agree and they nod their heads
this year it's the blue-reds
they smolder and she blows
on them and they smolder
even more.
but this minority.
holds out the way skin
holds out on the lips
and then gives in.

Mysteries of the Great Plains

i

What Immediate Effect did the Great Plains have upon the Anglo-Saxons?

Morning hangs in the valley, above damp clumps of aspen, trembling. Figures move along high bluffs, indistinct in the river mist, carrying canoes, bundles wrapped in rope and leather things. The trail is filmed with frost; treacherous. Below them water shatters in a throat of stones. Their mouths are taut. At the rear of the party is a man with a cocked hat and a sextant. Behind him are two Indians carrying a stretcher. There, wrapped in swaths of frost-stiffened furs, his fingers clutching a notebook, lies an incapacitated Peter Fidler. He has sore feet. A disquieting odor of bitumen is rafted through the valley on the fog.

ii

Did man originate on the Plains or in the Forest?

At their dig, where they have successfully recovered the skeleton of an animal previously unrecorded in this country, the paleontologists are having a party. They stand, in gowns and black tie, beside a fire on the pebbled flats of the valley. Some friends whom they have not seen for a long time have come down from the city for the occasion. Canvas tents are pitched in the shadows at the base of the valley wall. Between the tents and the river are piled like discarded styrofoam the bones of the old animal wrapped in plaster of paris. A barge is lying in the river. Firelight licks between the slats of crates stacked on the barge. As the paleontologists toast each other and their most recent find the rope slowly unravels.

And the barge floats out of the light in the slow disentangling of the river.

iii

Why is the West considered Spectacular and Romantic?

On the front porch sit an aluminum ladder, some asphalt shingles, batts of insulation and a pair of muddy boots. Rain is being driven in through open windows. The bundles of shingles have been thrown on the batts of insulation to prevent them from blowing away. Although they have been placed as far from the window as possible, the boots have filled with water.

Two young women come out of the house onto the porch. They are wearing laced camisoles and they throw themselves, laughing, upon the insulation, wrenching handfuls of fibreglass from the wet batts. When they embrace they place a batt of fibreglass between them. They take the shingles off the insulation and the wind lifts the batts across the porch like helpless birds. The women wad fibreglass into their mouths and slide the ladder out the window.

iv

Why was the West considered Lawless? Was it really Lawless or did it merely Appear Lawless?

The Saskatchewan Roughriders are running through offensive drills on the prairie southeast of Calgary. It is an away game. There are no yardsticks or hash marks. They are trying to get their timing down. After every play the coaches, one of whom stands in front of the centre, the second slightly behind and to the left of the setbacks, can be seen writing vigorously in their notebooks. A crowd has gathered at the roadside several hundred yards away, watching through binoculars. There is no sound except the slap of plastic on plastic, muffled in flesh. They are operating out of an I formation. The quarterback has called a slant off left tackle. He gives to the second man through. For an instant, a gaping hole is created in the line and the back slashes into it. The defence is nowhere to be seen.

v

Why is the West politically Radical?

The train is carrying a load of green lumber to Toronto. Somewhere, a spark has escaped from an overheated bearing, setting the plastic that wraps the stacks of plywood and 2x4s, masonite and chipboard, ablaze. Although the wood is green, it burns fiercely. It is midnight. The train drags a plume of fire across the flat land, the lumber warping in the heat, sap oozing from the planks, boiling. 2x4s spill off the car, tumbling over and over through the autumn fields like the rigid legs of huge metallic insects. Plywood rips off the stacks, settling in sheets of flame upon the swaths. When the train stops at the next town the burnt cars are unhooked and left to smolder at the siding. The town does not have a fire department. It has been named after G.U. Ryley, once a surveyor for the CNR.

vi

What has been the Spiritual Effect of the American Adventure in the Great Plains on Women?

It is midsummer. She goes braless. Among the landscapers there is a bet as to what color her nipples are. When she bends over to lay sod they stand in front of her, hoping to see down her t-shirt. Dust on her skin, the sweat weaving through it like the loose threads desire always is for those whose work ends in the fall. In September they were going to hold her down and roll the t-shirt above her breasts. So she showed them, glistening with sweat and dirt, and cried. They bought her lunch, a Big Mac and a chocolate shake, and she took the afternoon off.

vii

In Conclusion, let us inquire what has been and what is to be the Meaning of the Great Plains in American Life?

On the wall of the living room is a velvet painting of a covered wagon in the desert. There is a huge copper sun in the top left corner of the picture. Spikes of weathered rock cast shadows in an unmistakable profile onto the canvas. As if there was a face behind the painting. When she got her divorce she left this piece with her parents because there was no room in her small apartment. They said someday you'll want it back but she has forgotten. The dust from the covered wagon, painted with a vigor apparent nowhere else in the painting, coats almost everything.

Thermostat

small things: glass
        blooms, curtains
        swell with air, a
        spring tightens on the wall

she stands on a register in
front of the window and
waits for the heat to go on

outside
                it hurts to breathe

and where she stands, imperceptibly,
air
        bends steel

The Dream of Snowy Owls

i

Slow wings. The arrival
late in October, of snow.
It begins and you have
never learned to expect it
because nothing changes
fast enough. Love,
wisdom, weather.
Owl on a pole

ii

From the overpass north to the beaverdam is eight miles of meander, deadfall. They got up and put a hard white wax on their skis and broke trail up the creek. Moonlit snow. Stitched by shadow from the bare willow branches. Once they heard an owl and stopped. Twice they found the end of tracks. Shit, green bark in the scrub, rosehips with a faint red still in them like wineglasses left on the night-table, gnawed. The rabbit flushed, then wings.

They remembered angels. How they fell into fresh snow backwards and tried to get up and walk away in their old footprints. No unnecessary marks. But now sweat glues everything to them, layered clothing, the quilted snow, and they need motion to release them. Shivering, they turn towards the overpass, going back as snow comes in through gaps in black poplar along the bank, flakes collapsing as petals collapse off the cherry tree in their garden, not in a hard frost but in the sunlight afterwards. Two miles out she broke a tip and had to walk the rest of the way.

iii

he rarely dreams
but dreams owls. fixed eyes. snow
on the highway.

they refuse to move, perched
on shattered roadkill with intestines
in their beaks, the brown
bands deep across
breast and wing
not the immaculate birds of midwinter
but spring, the hollow
bones brooding with instinct

ready to fly
north.

driving, he would brake, swerve, barely
miss them
and they were indifferent

the first one he hit hardly moved.
he did not think to look back.

but they walked under the wheels, owl
after owl, feathers, pillows
broken
an airless room
and in his hands, no feeling
he would peer in the mirror
and discover them whole
unruffled
pivoting their heads
to watch him
disappear.

in the end it was deliberate. steering
at them, his foot rammed
with belief against the floor.
he rarely dreams and when he does
— the dreams wake him.

moonlight
sheers

frost

unfolded
on the glass

iv

in the summer they are gone.
he sleeps with the window
open and sweats into the pillow.
in the school library, an owl
mounted on a cut maple, a patch
of rabbit fur in its talons.
the librarian cannot remember
who donated it.

v

early March, driving
home from the city
in a wet snow, an

owl, caught in the solid
light, lifted
so slowly from the shoulder

no feather, no
wing, just a thud
on the glass, an imagined

flailing behind him now
tho he returned to
look, the snow

melting
inaudibly
on the pavement

vi

undreamt, the owl
flies from the pole
or does not fly
                                        that
there are wings, silent,
held, among curtains, glass,
a body of light persistent
in snow, a particular
symmetry

that the owl, at
least, assumes air
and the air
embraces it

from

The Alternate Guide

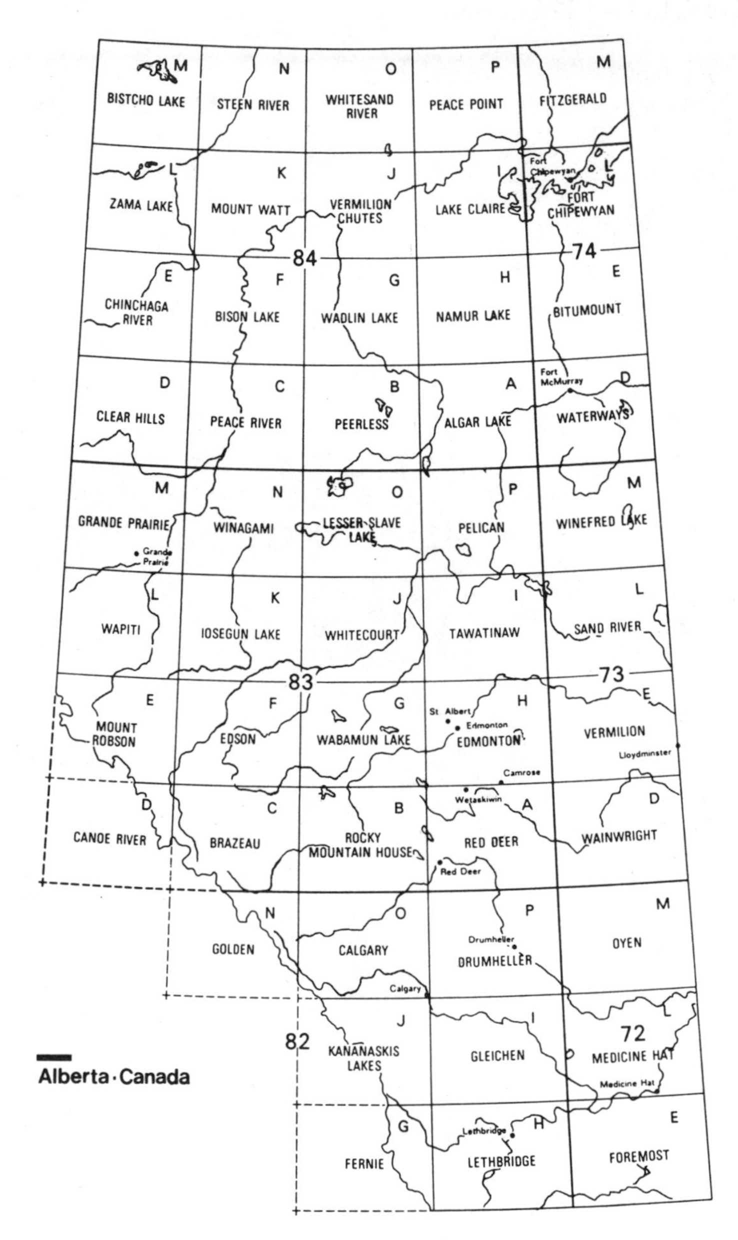

Alberta · Canada

How to Use This Book:

if you know the name of the place
use the index

if you are visiting, use the map
do not think of yourself
and another, think

of bigger numbers
the slash of either/or
is not empty, it is the mark

of a third party, another
terrain, insistent
and small enough to fit

in your car
carry it with you

72E 14 8 78

water freezes and
the molecules go
orderly

symmetrical flakes
drift into a
night we balance in

held
in a perfect
lattice

flesh, a local
knowledge

the hydrocarbon
bond
                and

snow
netted in
your hair

melting there
without authority

72L 23 11 80

a river
runs through the dead
through the porous

marrow
a drift of silica
that hardens

harder than
the actual
bone

femur
tibia
ilium

the stone remains
exposed
along a gully

as it ages
the dead are
what is known

standing
in relief
along the wall

ribs that cage
a stone
viscera

the solid waters
of a heart
the earth is

washed away from

73D 4 8 80

to give this moment
the minute

presented
snatched out of
memory, snow

suspended in a still
air
driving home

Christmas
Alberta to Saskatchewan
how at the meridian

an hour
slips away, a flake
caught on the tongue

and is held
out of habit in
the mind, always

an hour late, for
our return

73E 12 2 79

it is called
the Hill
of the Horns

from a singular
stone on top
of it

says James Hector
1859
but there is no

singular stone
Hector
never climbed

the hill
though he named it
having tea

and hard pemmican
with wandering
Cree, a misinterpreted

word, or so
we surmise
hunting

among multiple hills
for some trace, some
indentation

that would hold
this given
name

this disappearance
of stone

73L 23 2 79

forgiveness
is an appearance
that floats

on a semblance
of water

Floatingstone Lake
this rock
torn

from its formation
set by ice
here

called an erratic
but the error
as always

is human
the Crees called
it assinkagana

the stone
that floats

and we
as we do
all history

repeat
this ignorance

and
this grace

74D 24 7 80

crescent
                    the migratory
dunes, grain lodged

upon grain
   a drift of
shadow, honey

                         colored
light, the slopes
     a body

                whispers
a wandering trees
  are planted to contain

all this debris
detritus carried off
a lake

by wind, blown

kisses

82J 12 7 81

the rain forgets
its falling
as my oblivious

body
falls unmeasured
towards you

clouds seeded
full of silver
dust

blossom in a horizontal
air, dark
cumulus gathered

by the finite
particles rain needs
to coalesce

into a memory, a
weighted form, and then
the rain forgets

as tho it forgot
its own descent
the flowers

gather
mute and circumscribed
to break

and the earth
leans upward
to startle it

82N 15 12 78

the river
is a woman
who

says nothing
who braids her
hair, three

strands held
in such practised
fingers, such

sureness
no mirror
accounts for

she shakes
her head to toss
the braids

around her in
the wind that comes
down hills

and is gone
into the noise
of a valley

loved surely
past design

82O 21 2 79

the night is a fist held
around us
as if we were some

handle: a hoe
a spade, something
to turn the earth

into itself, not
an ideal garden but
a recognized

terrain, topos
calloused with
starlight

and full of unpractised
hands, unable
to straighten

our cramped fingers

83F 24 10 78

the pond's
surface
tension

supports the
water-strider's
glide

words
fragile as
insect legs

skim across
your nervous
skin

almost two
dimensional
without

response
to height
or depth

the water-strider
can't swim
and

if he breaks the tension
and becomes submerged

he drowns

83G 23 10 78

at night
while the garden
retracts its color

your arms
are like a
greenbelt

proposed
to keep the air
constant, full

of life
around a city
no longer lived in

to ring that world
with residence, a
common air

but the city
sprawls

we walk
in the garden

arm in arm
almost color-blind

83L 10 8 78

the heart
runs
from the hand

like those alpine
insects who die
from body heat

when you touch them

crystal peels
from the roofs of
ice caves

with the introduction
of human warmth

we bring heat
the way flames
lick the white spruce

bare
in the forest
the trembling

aspen
ring a shallow pool
the heart

in this succession
at the peak
of summer

a pool the
air transforms
and floats away

83O 19 9 78

introduced to New York
City: 1890

recorded in Alberta:
          1934

the starling sits with its
reputation for thievery
in a tree

mimic, a record
of stolen song, the voices
of a dozen others

exploited
into a history
the markings

of unclassified
birds
          and the starling

after it takes the song
from other birds

takes their nest

84E 17 12 78

they have found
the remains
of a squashed bird

bones
embedded in rock
a trace of feathers

from this they
postulate the origin
of flight

I believe we
come from
monkeys

that birds
are kin to
reptiles

that memory
will hold
your body

the impression
of wings

feather in rock

your hypothetical
touch

84F 8 11 78

you were like none of these:

the tongue of hound's tongue
beard of goat's beard
foot of goose foot

not the strife in loose strife
rue in meadow rue
or the wind in wind flower

the bed in bedstraw
foam in foam flower
either term in pussy toes

not prickly pear
touch me not
or skull cap

anything in blazing star
witch's butter
monkshood

unlike even the pale
death camas fringing
the sloughs

especially

84J 9 8 78

the cat stares
from the refinished
rocker you found in

a granary
took the struts
and arms apart

and took them
down to the dunktank
at your brother's shop

stripped them bare

they lie like bones
all winter on our basement
floor

                    only
the living
recall the dead

the chair sits with
its soft grain by
a fern hung

in a corner without traffic
too antique to use
except for the cat

whose weightless eyes
flare
with its delicate

possession

84L 3 10 78

water
finds a way
from its basin

the river
fills its channel
with silt

and invents
another course
the lake, closed

off
dies, choked
with milfoil, a

dream of permanence
here, camping
among colonies

of typical weeds
we wash our hands
before supper

and throw the
water into bush
around

an impatient shore

84N 3 2 79

great gray owls
can locate the sound
of a moving mouse

under snow 18 inches
deep at a distance
of 50 yards or

more and flying
low to the exact spot
they plunge feet

and head into
the drift to grasp
their prey

what commentary, what
ecology, comes
after this

beneath the snow
red-backed voles drive
shafts

towards the air

84P 14 7 78

rain

again

we build roads
and the roads
disappear

washed into ditches
culverts, creeks
into a lake

that seeps
into a river
and the river

where it spills
into a bay
leaves a

delta
alluvium
the shape of

a heart

at night the
porch roof under
our window is a shell

the rain whispers
in
and we lie there

listening
to the wash
of our breath

in an ocean

from

These Lawns

The Fern

Begin with instruction: the fern hung down to the floor and
you had to keep adjusting the planter, sticking

old catalogues under it, raising it higher and higher as the fronds
leaned out and down in tense arcs, all the individual

leaves dotted underneath with spores and turning
brown on the edges where they touched the carpet.

You must have done something
right, maybe the regular soakings with rainwater

collected in old tubs out back, or maybe
the music, simple melodies your pupils repeated so

often everyone left the house; the fern didn't
have a choice, and look how well it's done, it

hangs down to the floor and all you can do is
clip it back because you can't set the pot any higher.

That care keeps the fern alive, and simple, even tho at
your age it would be easy to forget and hard to reach

up with water, the fern keeps demanding your attention, above
the claims of all other plants, the ivy grown twice

around the room, held up with pins, the hoya, violets, lily,
all those I never will know the names of — they claim you too

the way they think the sunlight is theirs and
it is. The fern also needs light, tho it sits out

of the direct afternoon sun and dips its fingers into
sunlight puddled on the rug, tentatively; it

can't resist. And where it touches the rug
the leaves curl up and die and yet something

is nourished, new fronds uncoil downwards, nonflowering,
and I have often wondered why, among all the blossoms

that fall silently open throughout the house, so that
every morning surprises you with color, why you have loved

the uncomplicated green of this fern that has done nothing
except endure and now occupies half

the dining room. Is it the persistence that you love, that
one plant survives everything you can do to it

even love, it stays green and now there is nowhere
for it to go except out.

Just kidding.
All I wanted to do was describe the fern

for you, attend it with words, with something that will
also survive your love and not be anything else

to extend alternating leaves down into sunlight
at the front window. I wanted the fern to be nothing

else because you are so much like it, a patient green set
just out of the sun, unexplained except by care, how

it makes the room full, tho it has no spectacular flowers
that give themselves to comparison. The fern

has no flowers at all and will have none. But there is
this: after caring for it longer than I can remember, for

so long that even you cannot recall where you got it, you
probably didn't know its name comes from the word

for wings.

Dressing Mannequins

She has daughters, she tells herself, not
that it matters. Among the limbs, the rows
of heads, she puts a body together. She

has daughters, she tells herself, who could
wear these summer fashions that leave so much skin
exposed, that fit tight around the bodice. They are

so beautiful.
They wait for her, disjointed, staring
in contempt at the glass, they have been through

this before. And she almost holds the bodies
of her daughters in her hands, their sun
dresses and ribbons, how they could never sit

still. She sticks an arm into its socket, pins
fabric around a motionless waist.
It is never complete.

Even when she joins the window-shoppers and stares
in from the far side of the glass at these fashionable
women who are not her daughters, whose disdain

for those nothing will fit is made harsh and
immobile by floodlights, she knows ways
to improve it. She knows they are talking

tho she cannot hear them, about Tokyo, New York, Milan,
that they invent her every night, maternal
and made of easy syllables. She can see their lips

purse around her name, as if they had more
to say and were only waiting for the pedestrians
to pass. And she buys clothes

for her daughters, who can wear almost anything,
remembering their sizes, but never
at the store she works at.

Desire Lines

i

To get it right, desire lines are shortcuts in the grass,
the reality of dead lawn where too many people have walked.
In the jargon of landscape architects is something like belief.

Or perhaps it is just a topography made for us, some image
of ourselves, radiating as if from a center and even though the sod
has just been laid, its edges drying and beginning to pull apart,

and all the signs say keep off
we walk on it anyway. The grass dies and needs to be replaced.
More than anything, I am impressed by such orthodoxy.

ii

In winter, mule deer scuffle at sage and willow along the frozen
river bank. Their complicated stomachs, a friend explained, are what you
get when you eat grass. Their tracks gnaw across an unmade land.

An indigestion of tracks. Against necessity,
what endures of desire?

iii

Even love forgets, the way they truck pallets of evenly cut earth
in from a sodfarm on the outskirts and kids go by
leaning out car windows hollering
'green side up' and everyone hopes it will rain

so where they have stepped on it, nothing shows. I remember little of being a landscaper. How once we buried a shovel and laid the sod over it, don't ask me why. How we left tools behind, their handles weathering and expanding in the rain.

How only the most persistent of shortcuts, so many footprints, so many goodbyes, will be visible and even those, not until spring. Red fescue, kentucky blue, a few words.

Everything else, I guess, I love.

iv

I saw an old woman planting flowers all over her front yard, stubbornly. All their neighbors had lawns. When it rained mud washed down across the sidewalk and people had to step around.

Later, alyssum unlocked the cracks of the sidewalk. I saw
the old woman digging it out with a trowel. She had not wanted, she said, to sow such doubt.

v

Desire is the shadow
cast by the body's honest labor, it comes along
behind the visible and tromps down the grass and when we stop
it stands off in the distance, waiting, like a door, or an airport

that can be approached but when entered just becomes
the image of some place else, another place that might
also have desire in it, so we disappear into our own longing,
as if it were a package tour

and even that has become unaffordable,
so it is the work, and the patience, that are believable, as the deer,
too, cut a path through the clumps of speargrass
and the mud, making their way down to the river to drink

in the flat water just before dawn, they lift their heads,
the scent of someone on the path behind has reached them.

vi

The actual traffic goes, it thinks, only where it wants to go.
Ignoring sidewalks and willing to get its feet wet, there is always
another place it needs to get to sooner.

And sooner or later, the grass grows back, long spikes of it filled with silica
and dew. It recurs among fences and surrounds walls and there
is no way to tell where it stops.

Beside the garage, where I threw a plank last winter, the grass was
white and ingrown. Beneath the ground, it holds
the dead together obstinately.

What to Do with Orange Peels

the sweet
oranges

break open
because she
does

break them

in the given
light

a fire made
of newspaper
dry birch

in the brick
fireplace
where

she has laid
them the thick
peels

burn green

Another Trade

Something survives loss. A man steps onto the ice in an empty arena where arc lamps flicker high among girders and catwalks but the ice surface glows as if a light came through it, softly, from underneath. The man steps onto it. Takes two strides and coasts, wanting to see parallel lines, a discipline, when he looks behind him. Circles, faster and faster, the only one out, wanting to see himself reflected in the safety glass as he cuts hard behind the net, one leg over the other, but the glass is black and he stops, puffing, to lean on the boards in front of the timer's box. There is no image he could call his own, just the pale

visibility of shadows etched in the ice, artificial, the marks of earlier workouts, flooded over and preserved, so that every line is part of a challenge to appear, which is happening now, still, as the janitors move above him, high in the blues, sweeping up debris from the last home game, and if they called to him his name would skid down through the darkness like a wrinkled program thrown in disgust from the stands, but there is no sound, no autograph to sign, and he begins to skate again, stops and starts, head down between the bluelines, until the entire ice is cut with what is left of his disappearance.

Icicles

the intent
is clear: they

want to fall

at night you
lie awake
and listen

to them break
from the eaves

if they want
to fall

let them

Look Under Beauty

look under beauty, she
said, that's where I always
look when I want
to get my hair done

so I have spent hours
alone in the yellow
pages, not knowing
which to choose

Sutra for Brinkman in Nepal

i

Sometimes a man steps into the same river more than once.
It is the same because he steps into it.

Sometimes a man steps into the same river only once.
It is the same.

In April the ice went out. It broke and its echoes split
against the rocks. A thick green water ate its belly.
Every hunger is the same as this.

ii

Among the absurd peaks people live forever
on a diet of barley and goats' milk. They watch the scree
and rattling water this side of a glacier they say has never moved.
The other side of the glacier, they say, is more glacier.

While you were away, we went out to East Coulee
for breakfast. It was the usual, pancakes and eggs and ham
and afterwards we walked by the river that is the same as it was
when you left.

The cottonwoods along its bank are in leaf
and even their leaves have rivers in them, old drainage.
Even your hands are full of water. Everything is like a river, Don.
I remember you stepping into it, knowing it would be cold.

iii

By analogy, your feet are two old amphibians
whose bones you would like to bleach and measure
and give two-part latinate names

They are quiet and cold-blooded and you could ignore them.
But someday they could fly.

And for now, nothing else fits into your footsteps
as well.

iv

High in a mountain gorge
you found a stone where the river begins and it
came to you that if time is recycled, it is just so much junk.

The air thin and so dry
and inside the stone fossil clams meditated insolubly
about the meaninglessness of your trek.

Throw that stone away.

v

You came back and told us that in the water
live neglected demons. We showed you where the ice
had piled onto the shore and flattened the willows
and then disappeared, just like last year.

And now, in the heat of July, you can set up
a lawn chair in the mud of a sandbar and watch
great blue herons nest in cottonwoods on the far side
of the river you will enter again.

You call this neglect?
The willows slowly unbend, as if a wind lifted off them.
Their bark is red and scarred, although it is nothing
like the Asiatic rhododendron forests and their ghostly blossoms.

There is nothing supernatural about it.

vi

If they told you the earth was held up by a turtle
standing on the back of a dozen elephants
would you believe them?

When you come home you will forget,
whether you believed or not, says the permeable river.
There is no life before this one, says the suspended quartzite.

Your footprints are hung in the sea, piece by piece.
As they settle they are filled again, with water.

February 12

to have sent the heart discreetly, in plain wrappers, walking
in the wind to a mail box on the corner, to entrust it: an address, some

destination, the red postal trucks that shuttle
in the streets like heartbeats I could have said, noting the federal

colors, red and white, the necessary codes

to have sent the heart with its discourse, the long
explanations, cut out of a sheet of similar designs, impatiently, saying

be mine, with a special card for the teacher

there is nothing beyond comparison, the wind, here
in February, smug in the endless patterned drifts, among old

envelopes and Kleenex from knocked-over garbage cans, caught in
rigid hedges across the alley, or teachers crazy in their rooms, even

the post office, the heart slowed down in its sleep

and I have sent this to you, among a handful of letters, to explain
nothing is delivered on time in paradise, walking

to the mailbox against the wind, hoping this will get to you
in two days

Bird Not Singing

We have not yet learned to hate ourselves well enough.
The bird with pale breast feathers leans towards a mirror
hung in its cage. A boy is coaxing it to sing. He taps a bell,
whistles, and the bird flaps against the plastic-coated bars.
Stupid bird, the boy says.

In a basement room the boy is crying. For
himself, his father says. For myself, says the boy, knowing
nothing he says is true. I hate it all: school, the meals you cook,
the books you want me to read, this bird not singing.
Look how he yanks the feathers from his chest.
They settle on the floor, on newspapers covered with shit
and husks and gravel, shapeless down plucked from so close
to the body, so light any movement in the room lifts it
and it almost flies.

The bird sleeps, puffed, the air
retained by its body. The father sits at a window overlooking
a street where snow is falling in hard dry flakes the cars
catch and scatter, only there is so much of it eventually the traffic
stops. He is thinking of prisoners, those jailed because there is
a world that detains nothing except those whose words haunt
men who do not hate themselves well enough, who have
pistols and electricity and say tell us everything.
Talk. The father is thinking of how they slept, in
cold cells, expecting to be dead. He is thinking
of how they have probably never seen snow.

Late, he goes to watch his son sleep, stopping in the doorway
with the hall light on. The bird flutters in its cage but the boy
is still, his breath steady against the wall he turned to in anger
as his father walked from the room, earlier, turning the pain
in on himself. And even the father sleeps, though he does not expect it,
it falls on him like feathers at the bottom of a cage. And they have all
slept this sleep, the bird with its need to hurt itself, the boy's
anger, men with their words. What can you say
about this sleep except that it is done and we awoke
and dreamed nothing. We never dream.

Is that what a boy wants on a morning crisp and white as new sheets
and he is the first one to leave the house. When the trees are
puffed up with hoar frost and the father watches him: new
boots, new snow. How last night, a feather lifted from the cage
by a current he could not feel come through the door, fell
silently, relentlessly, towards him.

Working with Shale

You can't rush when you're working with shale, it crumbles.

And so you inch the rock saw's thin circle of teeth through
the slab, cooling it with a stream of dirty water, and when the
gridwork is complete, chisel underneath and pry the square
of rock from the old riverbed.

The giant footprint blooms in it.

As downstream the new dam backs the water up, solidly, and
the tracks disappear, one by one, under a current that comes
to them as a breeze silted with pollen.

They wait for it to pass among their unburied stamens
as you salvage what there is for memory: photos, sketches, casts,
even the sliced-up rock packed carefully on a jetboat.

What would it take to make you believe.

Even in the museum, where a footprint hangs on the wall
and you can place your palm within it, so small, even though
its pulp and gristle strain to reach the edges of this
imprinted thing, this thing no one could rush with, just a rock

you say, imagining it as motion, the stress
of a river disappearing, and then your hand feels bigger, as if it
too, with its dense cells, vascular, was just movement arrested
momentarily, and you say maybe it's possible but you doubt it.

Someone once suggested that the rise of flowering plants
caused the extinction of the dinosaurs but you know
now this could not be the case because how would it account
for the survivors.

It is a question you ask whenever there are survivors around:
what accounts for them?

In the shale beneath the river an index of simple animals
settles in the backed up current.

It dies in the rock with everything it had to say deferred into a past that is just a way of filling in a footprint after what made it is gone, some kind of repetition, a whispering of the story again, again.

Only survivors have one. Past. Index. Footprint. Again.

When you saw the footprint slab hung on the wall did you notice
the cracks, those hinges where your whisper inserts itself
like water and for a moment, a flower blossoms in this plenitude, as
empirical as only your distrust can make it.

Watching the Eclipse

I had expected more darkness, something abrupt.
The light on the walls stoops down towards benches
in the court where secretaries fed sparrows all summer
but now the snow is the only thing eating, it chews
at the concrete and wrought iron and breaks the twigs
of ash and honeysuckle where the birds wait for berries.
I had expected measure, not the imperceptible fading,
the light stretched thin down the sandstone facings,
the body gone out of it.

Memory is just a film we watch this eclipse
through, protective, to see the edge of something pass
through the light. I know you sit upright in the recliner
in the dimmed living room, among the small trophies,
the photo albums, the gifts your students left for you,
inadequate reminders, staring out at the snow-covered
garden, thinking the baby's breath and poppies
there all summer. This hole in the middle of the literal
heart. Afraid to lie down because the ribs tighten in their orbit
and every variation no longer feels like sentiment
or irony but something more urgent, more contemporary.

I called you and you told me you'd seen the eclipse, the last
one this century, without mentioning you'd been in the hospital
at all. Here, the light just touched the floor of the courtyard
when the moon's shadow carried past it. I watched it, then
threw the piece of film away. It is always as if the attention
wanders, as if concentration would have made the sky
darker, more birds roost, totality. That word
scares me. I know some people travelled
around the world for this but I no longer
need it. We no longer need it. Any of us.

Think of yourself, nothing else has the clarity of self-pity.
I guess we shared this eclipse and I could have seen it
with more clarity. And now, in spite of myself,
I know a woman whose heart is in shadow forever.
No, not forever. The sparrows
gather again in the bushes in the courtyard
and there are limitations in the world.

These Lawns

i

Eden must be pure surface, the uniform green of these lawns, upon which the decorative sprinklers flower, their blossoms a seep of alkali, pale salts, residue.

For which they hauled in wheelbarrow after wheelbarrow of fine river silt, mica-flaked, the light restless in it, knowing it would be full of weeds and easily compacted

and yet they thought this was required, the lawn somehow exhausted in spite of the asexual grasses, their roots, rhizome, filament,

probing through bentonitic clay towards deep rock, irretrievable as gossip.

As if all that talk was spliced to their cells as a kind of resistance to surface, and he could taste the salt on her skin that afternoon, saline, made out of their own effort, their own belief

dispersed.

And so they rebuilt the lawn and it came up intermittently and less than perfect, a fizz of strange grasses that clawed their way in from

a zone that may be specific but had not been planted, from some botanical materials reservoir beyond hedge and garage, stubborn with their memory of native prairie. It was almost vindictive the way they appeared among the delicate flare of new seed.

There is no
nature they could say they have,
and no intention in it, and no garden
in it either.

And yet, starting the lawn mower, between pulls, he heard the agitation of a yellow warbler in the lilacs, flickering as if it were early morning sunlight, and when he looked at the uncut grass, the blades bending over, he knew something there
made his loneliness impossible.

ii

He wanted to see her as the landscape. He knew a geologist who had cited this particular topography as "subequal mamillary hills."

The Rumsey Moraine contains the world's largest stretch of unbroken aspen parkland. In late June, its hills are green and yellow, adrift on warm, nutrient-rich currents of gama and bunchgrass. Yellow-headed blackbirds guard the sloughs, which are barricaded behind walls of cat-tail and young aspen stands. The aspen are in cotton.

"I don't know why they bother with seeds," she says, lifting a string of fluff off the surface of a hill. "Most aspens start by suckers. But they put all this white stuff out anyway. It almost never works."

"Just like people," he said.

Beyond the aspen stands is a meadow purple with three-flowered avens, and beyond that, slope after rootbound slope of prairie wool upon which the wisps of seed are caught with their futile lustre.

iii

He thought of each swatch of grass as velcro, as what stuck the edge of the planet to its atmosphere.

He thought of each hollow stem as a tunnel into the complicated dirt.

Perhaps they were the tubes through which something breathed. Hid and breathed, like in a movie, while on the surface the temporarily better-armed enemy prowled along the banks of the river.

He thought of the invisible but diagnostic flowers. Some grasses, he had heard, flower underground.

Love is a burrowing, he thought, recalling a botany course.

Culm, axil

 ligule, glume.

He thought of the tracks of subatomic particles photographed against an artificially darkened backdrop.

He thought of the nitrogen cycle, the carbon cycle, the hydraulic cycle. The bicycle.

There is always more than one wheel.

He thought of the coarse hair that had thickened, recently, on the solid panel of gristle and bone just below the nape of his neck.

It embarrassed him.

iv

It is not the singular that needs to be preserved but the habitable space itself. He cut the lawn.

The prairie may be the most threatened ecosystem on the earth

and yet it persists, even in the manicured and deadly gardens, or the disturbed areas, marginal

the way the Rumsey Moraine is both too hilly and too full of gravel, glacial outwash just below the skin of grass, breathing, or the patch of tallgrass prairie in Winnipeg, uncultivated.

This is the way he loved her.

New Poems

Calling the Owl

i

Two owls sat on fenceposts in a clearing just off the road. A strand of rusty barbed wire was all that held the posts up. One owl had flushed from the nest in a huge cottonwood as we walked beneath it. Otherwise we wouldn't have noticed. The smaller male came in, on powerful soundless wingbeats, to join it.

At first they watched us calmly. Then they began to call. It was unlike any sound we had ever heard. A mew and a howl, an undulating laugh, back and forth, one at a time, never interrupting. We were astonished, and in the falling dusk made uneasy by the recitation.

But we tried nonetheless to call back to them, imitating the sounds, trying to follow the rhythm, the pattern. The owls listened, their heads swivelling, ear tufts bristling. Abruptly, they lifted from the posts and disappeared into the evening. The old wire vibrated slightly.

ii

at the back of the throat, in its darkness,
gather saliva and whistle through it to produce the modulated shiver

the salacious talk, the call we practice to the other world, to trespass
and attract its attention

and as it comes to inspect the penetrated edges of its territory
it becomes for a moment visible

we see in the scoop of its face the chaste ghosts,
as it disappears on silent wings

iii

We tried to learn the calls from Audubon Society records and never mastered them, although in our anger over the years we did alternate silence with glottal accusations, as if this were the call of our species, its particular adaptation

to the unknown. For years, we would stand at the edge of the bush and hoot into the trees and sometimes there would be an answer, an inhuman snicker from the dark spreading trees beyond the willows. But nothing ever appeared and eventually we gave the practice up

thinking the owls mere omens, cultural veneer of death and wisdom, and one night when we saw a Great Horned perch on our neighbor's tv antenna, the breeze waffling its softened feathers, we looked at each other thinking there will be a death in the house but not wanting to say it and in the spring of that year there was.

iv
"then nightly sings the staring owl"
at the back of the throat, among its lost work

glissando of recollected notes
reputedly pitched in the key of E, like so many

blues, so much thrown
voice, so that where you are

is the *matériel* of nothing
mother of such unpredictable appearances

v
years later, late one night walking along a back alley in Mill Woods in a dry November snow the calls came back to me and I began to whistle them, hardly more than an owly gargle in my throat. Anyone who heard me would have thought I was crazy

when out of the corner of my eye I caught the shape materializing out of the darkness, the horned silhouette, on a fence in the falling snow. It was as if it had come to the edge of something, its territory perhaps, to watch, it sat so imperturbably still

and I stood still too, congratulating myself on my calls, how even here on the edge of the city I had drawn an owl. I stepped closer, expecting the bird to lift into the resiliant air but it didn't. Eventually I realized it was a ceramic lawn ornament someone had perched on their fence.

vi

did you think you would make the lawn ornaments dance behind you,
enchanted with the toneless imitation you say is a call?

can't you see them twitching into life, marching off the lawns of this suburb
and parading behind you: fawns and dwarves and flamingoes?

and yes, owls too, with their exaggerated idea of bulk
and the plumage that makes them disappear

vii

There may be an owl in my throat, but crows walk by my eyes.

Said an old woman in a black kimono in northern Japan whose eyes lit when she heard we were looking for owls. I thought of the eyeshine in the great birds, how they reflected light through their eyes twice, seeing you, and seeing you again.

The woman pointed to pine-covered rocks that massed between her ryokan and the sea. That afternoon we saw a dozen crows wheel around a perched owl until the owl could bear it no longer and fell into the air. The crows trailed behind like a sash of caws until it disappeared over a headland. Then the crows returned to the owl's perch and sat there silently, mourning.

Crows and owls, night and moon, flock and solitaire. I don't know anyone who tries to call crows.

viii

all material has the spookiness of the real
comes unmistakably from the mud

of our voices and sits
as an owl will sit in the palm of a young girl

as if it were fearless and unalive:
oh you protected ghosts, give us this recognition

in the fired ceramic of a lawn ornament
is the howl of clay

What We Call It

"The one who has arrived has a long way to go."
Tomas Transtromer

She used to call it "going."
Did you go, she would ask.

I always called it "coming."
Did you come, I worried.

She anticipated departure.
I was expecting arrival.

Not presence, just the
moment of getting there.

And for her, that moment
of disappearance.

In either case, whichever direction
ecstasy moved it

carried only an overnight
bag and a passport

with that awful photo.
Even so, we thought

we would recognize it
there in the waiting room

among the crowd.

A Perfect Audience

I need to talk to someone, desperately, simply because you
are not here to talk to.

I am afraid even my self-conscious silence will give me away.
It has always been a betrayal.

I need to talk to someone because I have not seen you for three weeks
and I need the reassurance that I am not imaginary

that I can construct an image of you out of the evidence of my senses, one
that has nothing to do with general principles or distance.

I need to talk to someone so I can imagine you have just left, which is
perhaps how I will always remember you

looking up from your car, or your hard heels thunking on the wooden deck,
keys in your hand, your smell on my chest.

I need to tell someone these things and in your absence the only person I
can tell them to is you.

If you were here silence would be the gap we are always putting
our mouths around, the space of our separation,

and I would admit this too, to someone, if there were someone to talk to,
who could be trusted not to spread it any further and could perhaps

celebrate with a quiet glass of wine, French, Californian, one that travels
well. In your absence I indulge.

I have been tempted even to talk to my wife thinking my joy would
outweigh her disgust and at the very least

she would be discreet.
Vanity, I told myself and kept silent. And it is

something you keep, unable to give it away, though I have tried
to paste it to the back of your mouth

with my tongue. It always comes loose. I find it in my pockets
superfluous as old Kleenex and I have stopped caring

how it got there. It has the texture of a ghost, the rind
of an apple. I never worried

about someone to talk to before but now I need to tell someone
She is remembered because she has always just left.

They will say she is coming to you, she is leaving the distant place,
Babylon, or one of Calvino's cities where desire rises up, some morning,

everywhere, as if it had to check the stocks in the paper before breakfast.
Someone could talk to me about this, just to fill the time

until you arrive. Silence, I have learned, is the easiest
to see through. They come into my office and say how come you're

so quiet and look at me as if I had a hickey on my neck and I go and
look and my body is transparent. Silence is another way

of talking to yourself. But I want an accomplice, one less pandering.
One who will insist on such a realistic image of you

that I have no choice but to believe it. One who knows nothing about you
except what I choose to tell. You may doubt the existence

of such a person, or suspect her motives. Sometimes I doubt your existence
too, although I have kept that very much to myself.

Apple blossoms, that's what I want to talk about. Apple blossoms, lost
earrings, a perfect audience.

Crabapples

for David and Corey

i

The small apples have pinched off the tree
and fallen in a ragged halo on the lawn, as if winter
shone from another side of the leaves and these tarnished
apples were the shadow's scatter.

The closer the light
the larger the shadow, until at some point we no longer
see the edge of what has been cast
among us and declare it, with all due gravity, a life.

ii

They do not belong to us, but to the light
that falls in the next yard, where the neighbors I recall
are gone, and the new owners newly retired and still
indifferent

although to them the apples shine like the flensed
skulls of every small animal that sheltered here.

Take as many as you want, they say.

iii

Even as we pick our way among them,
rake them into piles and gather them into the plastic bags
which we will take home to be stored in the deepfreeze
and emptied, gradually, for the winter birds who will find,
in the thawed juice and the seeds passing through them,
another reason to remain, the apples are luminous.

They lie self-satisfied upon the brown grass,
knowing each is proof for some substantial inheritance,
such as who is the most lovely, that would be passed on

through generations of their kind. The density
of such knowledge takes them almost through the earth
and still, you can pick them up, calm them as the troubled
fall light licks among their scatter and say, objectively,
you are merely apples.

Oh my literal-voiced sons,
I have not talked enough with you.
                    See the literal apples.
Sweet rot escapes their skin, and robins probe the broken cells
to hurry it along.

iv

The leaves don't matter, the young boys are told, as
they gather the apples into piles and scoop them, without
any mechanism of selection, other than that these apples
have fallen, into the bags.
                    The leaves have fallen too
and although none of the birds will eat them, they ease
each friction. They will be good company as the apples
jostle quietly in the deepfreeze
                    as if they were commuters
in a crowded subway car entering the last familiar tunnel
before their stop and knowing that their passage
is made up of just so much inadvertent light.

v

How many times have we made this trip
together, you and I, the herd of compass minerals that gather
on the tongue of this species to give it this particular density
and guide its migration, relentless in their shuffle.
They line up in our tissue and point towards the past and
once there, continue to point.

I know you have not loved
this trip, each year's eight-hour navigation to the small
Saskatchewan town and the rented farm and your eagerness
this year came unexpectedly. It made me happy, even though
I know you have come to watch an antecedent generation
thread its guilt and instinct together

how my mother
and I have shared, if at all, the quilt of daily uncertainties
now handed on to you with the rest of the bedding
and the knowledge you'll have to sleep in the basement.

How the father I claim not to have known makes his ghostly hobble
through the overheated rooms, points his cane at us and says
there is nothing you can do, nothing, to save me.

Can you understand it now,
my diligent anger, my love, the way we have always
collected the apples?

vi

Oh yes, they make good jellies, she says, if you have time
for that. Or if you can still reach up to pick them.

The tree
survives by letting its leaves go, or perhaps by letting go
the insubstantial smell of the apples, which must be taken in,
past the mucous, past the wavering cilia, and it hangs upside down
in the lungs all winter like migratory butterflies

and then must
return, which is why I toss open the windows each spring
and the tree takes back its blossoms from my metamorphosed breath.

As you smoothed the quilt across the guest room bed
did you hear her say that?

vii

Just the same, she does not recall how in those years I stole apples
from the same tree, creeping into the neighboring
yard to fill my pockets, then hid in the dust-lined ditches to pelt
teenagers in their waxed cars

She knew, because
the neighbors caught us one night and phoned her
and when I came in she asked to smell my hands
upon which, among the stains, was the undeniable tingle of apples
and yet, she does not recall.

So it will become a story
I can admit, gratefully, to my own children, to you. Unless
she has told this, for her own purposes, to you already
and you are waiting merely for me to confirm
what you have known for years.

viii

We collected so many apples we
had to give some away. We found a charity of deer
that had been feeding on the piles of grain, overabundant,
left beside the granaries on the farm.

We scattered a ring
of apples around the wheat, a preventive circle in the stubble,
as if the deer would be excluded, and within the charmed ring
the entranced wheat lapsed into sleep.

The man who rented
the farm shovelled them into the bush as soon as we left.

We knew that would happen, but I had wanted to show you
where I had seen a lynx sitting in a poplar fork one winter morning.
It was the only time I had ever seen one, wild. It was ghosted
with frost and when it finally moved, it was as if it shook
the glittering particles into a pure fog of itself
and disappeared.

The following spring
I built a treehouse in the same spot, perhaps for credibility.

And although the treehouse too has been torn down
I wanted to show you the branch, with old spikes rusting
in the scarred circle of bark, entranced and fragile with oxygen.

ix

We left the next day, packing the bags of apples
in the trunk of our car along with other mementoes
found in the farmhouse: an old straight razor identified
as my father's, the bowl of a cream separator that would
make a planter in a basement apartment, the boredom
that would absorb light like a stone in a windowsill
you eventually throw out.

                                        Not returning, one
forgets most quickly the boredom of returning
and, as one recollects where the stone came from
only vaguely, one forgets how quickly
one forgets.

x

          Some would say it is a boring road.
The flat stretch west of Saskatoon with its bleached stubble,
where there is always dust, or acres of storm or this time,
blind farmers and their depreciating trucks.

                                        Why I had been
expecting this I couldn't say, but was already slowing
down when the red three-ton with a full load of wheat
approached the highway and so skidded only briefly when
he pulled out in front of us
without stopping.

                    We sat half in the ditch, gasping.
In the trunk, the apples spilled, and their pungent breath
came around us eagerly.

Too eagerly.

xi

You will remember that trip. We have filled up the deepfreeze
and the softest apples are spread upon the lawn as if they were the
molts of small creatures that have crept into the mystery
of another shell.
The birds ignore them.
Although I have seen them on the evacuated branches of the trees
considering this emptiness between quick spurts of
themselves. The apples implode slowly, furrowed
the way a brow after years of cultivation is readied for new seed.

By the time of the first unrelinquishable snow the apples
are an amniotic slime and when your friends come through the gate
I can see them check their feet and hands, fearing
this is an odor others have smelled upon them
all their lives.

xii

All winter, our company reminded me of you, in your
distant rooms. It was not the birds that came,
but friends, salesmen, those who did not know you had moved,
and upon all of them was the redolence of these small apples.

I could smell it, even in the tracks of unknown visitors who stepped
briskly to the door as if they expected someone to be home
and walk away with equal confidence, knowing they can return.

Notes on the Poems

Karst Means Stone (NeWest Press, 1979)
Karst Means Stone is based on a memoir written by my grandfather, Samuel Karst. Originally of German descent, he immigrated, together with his family, to Canada from Russia in 1912. The memoir, which provides the quotations at the head of the poems, was written on a farm in Saskatchewan and is full of marriages and untimely deaths, of fires and crop failures and grandchildren.

To me it has always been a somewhat suspect document. It was written later in my grandfather's life and is, to some extent, an apologia for his strong religious views. My mother translated it and her protective instincts were also in evidence. The poems address what persists in the family even when the texts are unreliable.

The Life of Ryley (Thistledown Press, 1981)

The Dream of Snowy Owls (Longspoon Press, 1983)
Once, on the highway at dawn, I saw the sun's rays break through a cloudbank and catch the tops of a line of high-tension towers. Miles away, a white flare burned above one of the towers. It was a snowy owl. I have never seen anything as brilliant. Another time, driving in a spring snowstorm, we hit, just barely, an owl as it attempted to lift off the road's shoulder. We stopped and looked for it but it was gone. I have dreamt about it ever since.

The Alternate Guide (rdc press, 1985)
In 1979 I was employed by the Provincial Museum of Alberta to edit a field guide to the natural history of the province. Much of the material that had been collected had to be cut as the field guide took shape. *The Alternate Guide* is made up of poems that grew out of the extraneous material.

Both books are organized around the National Topographic System, a system of maps that represents Alberta with fifty separate mapsheets. The numbers of the mapsheets, along with dates of composition, provide the titles of the poems.

These Lawns (Red Deer College Press, 1990)
For the past decade I have worked closely with scientists in several disciplines. In spite of their arcane jargon and specialized journals they continue to maintain a great respect for the tangible world. There are, for instance, sophisticated mechanisms to determine deposition rates in ancient river channels, but a basic one still in use is to put a piece of rock in your mouth, letting your tongue sample the particle size. *These Lawns* tries to find room for both the jargon and the presence of the world.

New Poems
In order of their appearance here, these poems were originally published in *Fiddlehead, Dandelion,* and *Poetry Canada*. Thank you to the editors.